KW-328-573

My Mommy Put Me In The BASKET!

The Story Of Prophet Moses - Musa

Part One

Written By: Lilly S. Mohsen

Illustrated By: Ahmed Madbolly

MAC
Muslim Association of Canada

The Prophets To Islam Kids' Series

STARDUST

Published by Lilly's Stardust Production Inc.
Text copyright © 2012 by Lilly S. Mohsen
Illustration copyright © by Ahmed Madbolly

All rights reserved. No part of this publication may be reproduced, or transmitted in any form or by any means, electronic or mechanical, including photocopying, recording, or any information storage and retrieval system, without the prior written permission of the publisher.

Lilly's Stardust Production Inc.

My Mommy Put Me In The BASKET!
The Story Of Prophet Moses (Musa) Part One

The Prophets To Islam Kids' Series
Volume № 15

ISBN-13: 978-1481255905
ISBN-10: 1-481255908

Cover Designed By: Dina Soliman

Published in Canada by

Stardust Production Inc.

Printed and bound in Canada

Dedication

This book is dedicated to
Dr. Jason Mclean
One of the strongest swords of
Islam...
To the man who possesses
strength, faith and patience...
And is the true symbol of what
every Muslim man should be like...
May Allah bless you and your
beautiful family....
Amen....

Lilly S. Mohsen

Thousands of years ago, an evil king named

"Pharaoh"

ruled the great land of Egypt.

Everyone was SUPER SCARED of him!

One day Haman, the Pharaoh's advisor, gave the Pharaoh bad news.

"I had a dream that a boy will be born from the 'Bin Israel' tribe, and he'll take over your kingdom when he's older!"

Haman said.

The advisor's dream made the Pharaoh SUPER DUPER angry!

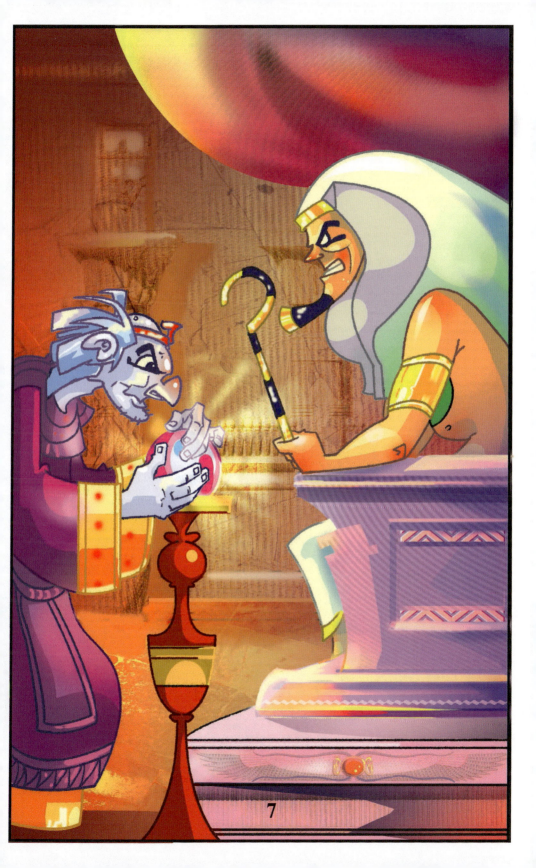

"WHAT DID YOU SAY?! TAKE OVER MY KINGDOM?"
The Pharaoh roared.

"I WILL NEVER LET THIS HAPPEN. I WILL ALWAYS BE THE KING!"
The Pharaoh roared even LOUDER
As he gathered his men.

"SPREAD THE NEWS! NO WOMAN FROM THE 'BIN ISRAEL' TRIBE IS ALLOWED TO GIVE BIRTH TO BOYS THIS YEAR!"
He yelled.

"I just gave birth to a baby boy!"
A sad mom from the 'Bin Israel'
tribe told her daughter.

The sad mom already had an
older son named Haroun, he was
saved from any harm because he
was born before the Pharaoh
made that new rule. But what
about her new born baby boy?

"What will I do now? The
Pharaoh said no women are
allowed to give birth to boys this
year!"
The mom said sadly.

"Oh my dearest baby boy!"
The mom whispered to her
baby, "How will I protect you
from the Pharaoh and his
men?"

Suddenly, she heard the
loveliest voice!
"If you're scared someone
might hurt him, feed your baby
from your milk and then put
him in a basket and cast it in
the Nile River."

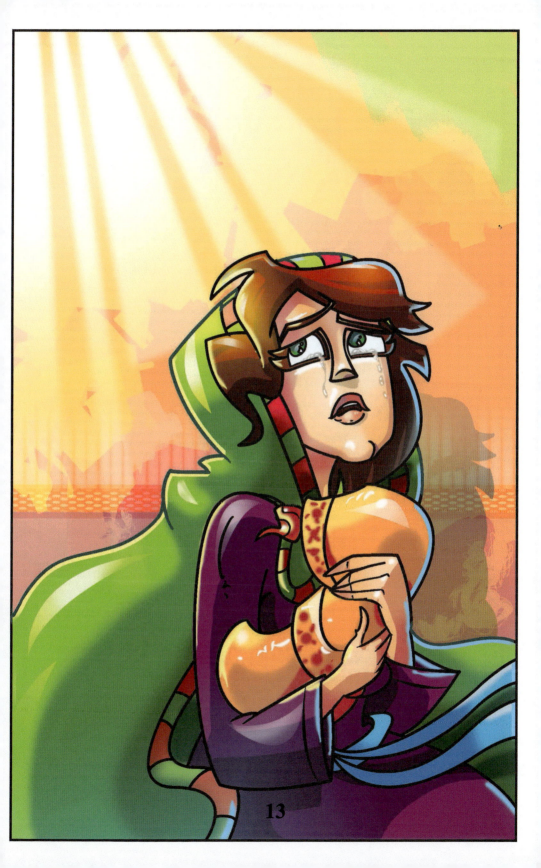

"Don't worry! Allah the Greatest will take care of your baby."
The lovely voice said.

"And please don't be sad, Allah will return your baby back to you."

"I trust Allah!"

The mom said as she kissed her baby and put him in a basket.

The mom gently placed the basket on the Nile River and left it to

FLOAT AWAY.

The baby's basket drifted down the Nile River, until it stopped in front of the PHARAOH'S royal palace!

"Look what I found!"

One of the Pharaoh's family members said, "There's a BABY in this basket! We better take it to the queen!"

The queen was very different from her husband, the Pharaoh.
He was evil and mean, but she was kind and caring.

Asseya, the Pharaoh's wife, held the baby and smiled warmly.

"What a beautiful baby! Please let me keep him!" She asked the Pharaoh. "Please don't hurt him! Perhaps we can adopt him as a son!"

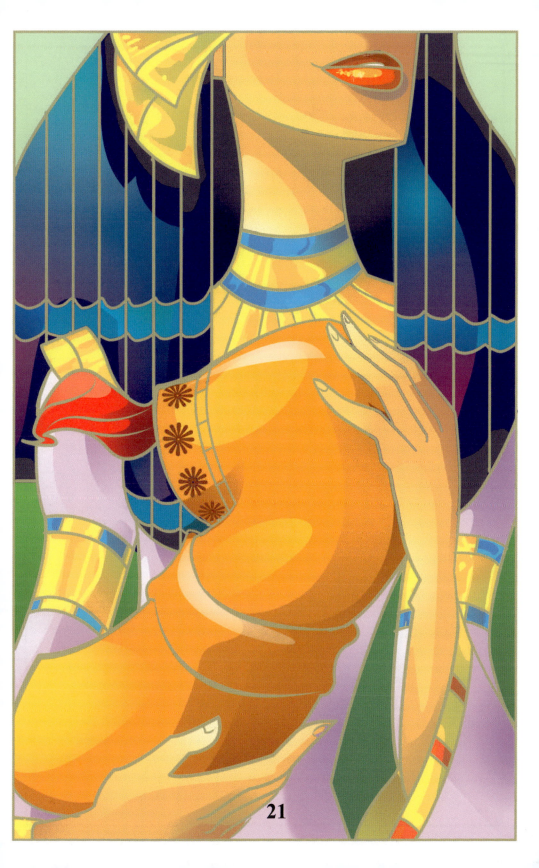

21

Allah placed the love for this baby in people's hearts. Even the Pharaoh agreed to let him stay in the palace and raise him as a son.

"I shall name him Moses!
Which means
DRAWN OUT OF THE WATER" The queen smiled,

"But who will feed him? We need a wet nurse!"

Back at home, Moses's real mom was so sad.

"Please go watch your baby brother from far. I need to make sure he's okay!"
She told her daughter sadly.

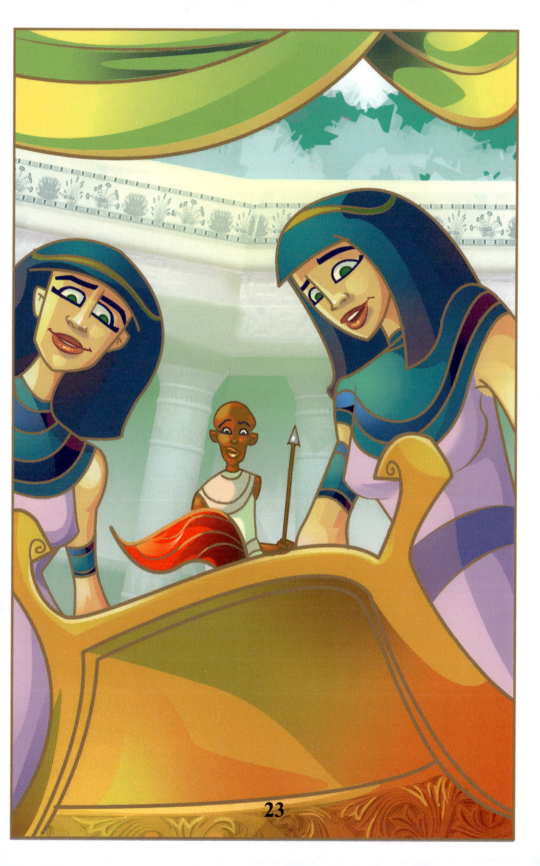

At the royal palace, baby Moses cried and cried! He did not want to drink the milk from any of the wet nurses that came for him.

"I know a wet nurse that can feed this baby!"
Moses's sister told one of the palace maids.

"Get her here now, please!"
The maid said.
"The baby is very hungry and our lovely queen is getting worried about him!"

"MOM! MOM!"

Moses's sister rushed back home.

"Oh honey, what took you so long?"

Her mom asked worriedly.

"You will NEVER believe this! My baby brother won't let ANY wet nurse feed him AT ALL! I told someone at the palace I know a woman who can! You can feed him, right?" The sister asked.

"Of course I can! He's my baby boy!"
Moses's mom ran outside happily.

The queen gave her baby Moses when she arrived at the palace.

"Allah brought us back together again, my sweet little boy!"
Moses's mom whispered happily.
"Allah is The Greatest, and always keeps His promises!"

Moses's mom fed her baby lovingly, and she was allowed to stay with him for as long as she wanted.

She didn't tell anyone in the palace that she was baby Moses's REAL mom.

SHHHHHHHH, it was a secret!

Moses grew up in the palace and became a VERY strong man.

Allah also gave him wisdom and knowledge! People came to him for help, and he always took care of the weak, the poor, and the old.

Moses visited his family all the time, and became close to his brother Haroun.

One day, as Moses walked in the garden, he spotted two men fighting. One was from the 'Bin Israel' tribe, and the other man was an Egyptian.

"Help me please! This man is beating me up!" The one from Moses's people cried out.

"HELP ME!"

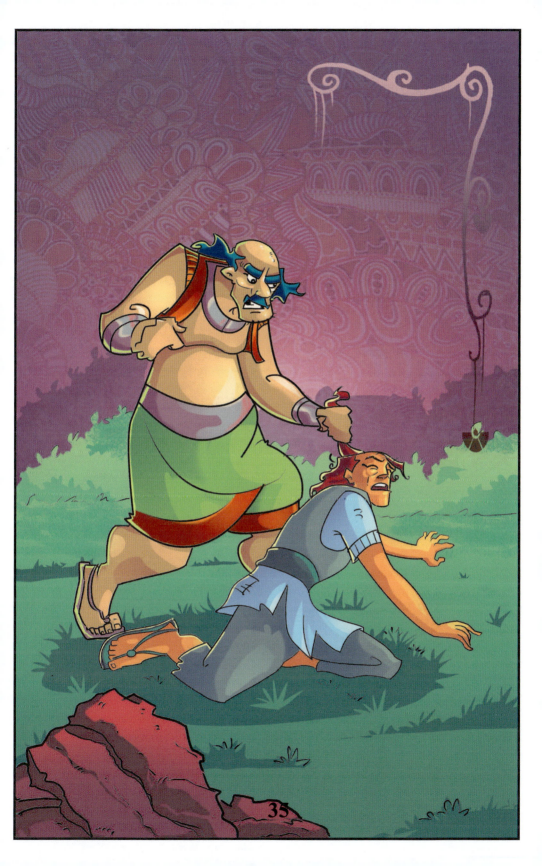

Moses got angry from all the fighting and yelling. He pushed the other man away to stop him.

"OH MY GOD! I think he died!" The man from Moses' people gasped.

"I just pushed him!" Moses was shocked. "I didn't mean to kill him! Oh dear Lord! This is the work of the devil, he's our misleading enemy!"

Moses was very sad. He didn't mean to kill anyone.

"Allah, please forgive me!" He begged over and over.

A little while later, a man came from the far end of the city to warn Moses.

"Oh Moses, some of the powerful people are planning to kill you! Leave the city now! I'm giving you my honest advice!" He said.

(Based on the meanings of Surat Al-Qaşaş Chapter 28, Verse 20, Holy Qur'an)

39

Moses was SUPER worried.

"Oh Allah, please save me from the wrongdoers!" Moses said fearfully.

Moses ran and ran in the direction of a city called 'Madyan'.

"Maybe Allah will guide me to the right way!" He said hopefully.

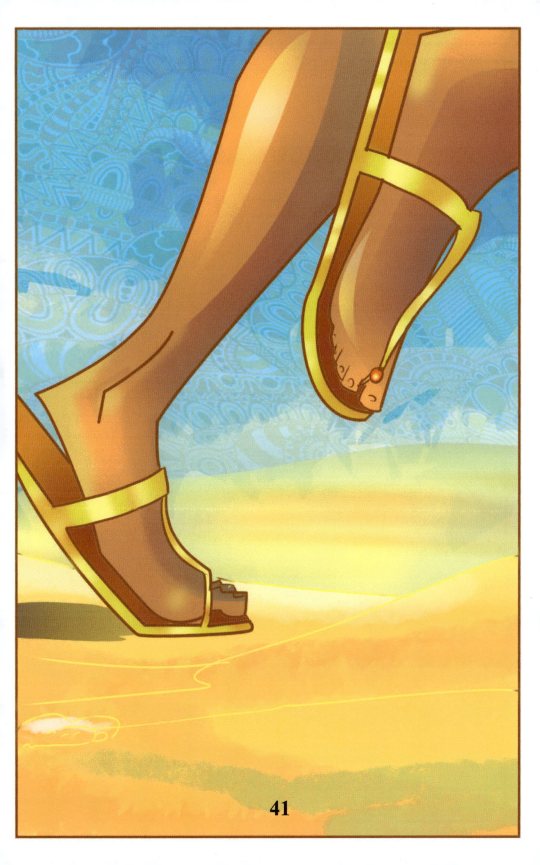

Moses finally reached the water well of 'Madyan' city. There, he found two young women standing on the side away from the crowd. The two women looked worried!
"What's wrong?" Moses asked them.

And that's when a whole new story started...

To Be Continued In Part Two: Did God Ever Speak To You?

ABOUT THE AUTHOR

Lilly S. Mohsen is the author of the "Prophets To Islam" series for children plus many others. Her books reflect the timeless message of the Holy Quran, and the valued morals we learn from those beautiful historical stories. Her most sacred wish is to open a new door for the young generation to help them see and feel the glory of our perfect religion... Islam.
Lilly studied Photographic Journalism at the American University in Cairo. She worked as a freelance writer and photographer for a number of magazines and agencies, till she finally decided to write her own books.
Lilly lives in Egypt with her son, Yasseen and her daughter, Magda, whom she proudly admits, are the main source of her inspiration.

"He who travels in the search of knowledge, to him God shows the way of Paradise" Prophet Muhammad (PBUH)

"Prophets To Islam" Series For Children"

For comments, please email Stardust Production Inc.
info@stardustproductiononline.com
www.stardustproductiononline.com